Fairy Kids and Kittens

Spinning Spider

Coloring with markers or other
wet media may bleed through to the
other side of the page.

The pictures in this book are printed on
black-backed pages so that any bleed-through
will be less noticeable.

Slipping a piece of scrap paper behind
the page you are working on will prevent markers
bleeding through onto the next coloring page.

Copyright © 2020 Rachel Armington

Please support independent creators' rights, and
do not participate in or encourage piracy of copyrighted material.

All rights reserved. No illustrations or any part of this book may be reproduced in any form by any electronic or mechanical means without written permission from the artist. It's illegal to scan, upload, or distribute any images of this book via the internet or any other method without written permission of the artist.

ISBN: 9798664463880

Published by Spinning Spider
SpinningSpider.com

Fairy Kids and Kittens Coloring Book

Rachel Armington

Contents

Ice Cream	15
Butterfly	17
Swat!	19
Visitor	21
Sofa Fairies	23
Violet Patch	25
Bath Time	27
Up in the Air	29
Hungry Mouse	31
Bad Kitten	33
Flower Box	35
Cheese and Crackers	37
Slender Branch	39
Hyacinth Girl	41
Hanging Around	43
Swinging	45
Catch Me if You Can	47
Jealousy	49
Fly Away	51
Kittens Think Oranges Stink	53
Four Friends	55
In the Trees	57
Dragonfly Kites	59
Wrestling Match	61
Kitten with Stripes	63
Climbing Kitten	65
Pounce	67

Free Falling	69
Singing Fairy	71
Cuddle	73
Rodent Rescue	75
Naptime	77
String	79
Fairy Leap	81
Climbing Buddies	83
Fashion	85
Storytime	87
Silly Fairy	89
Grumpy Cat	91
Tickle	93
Slide!	95
What's Up?	97
Fly Over	99
Daisy Chain	101
Tug of War	103
Kitchee Kitchee Koo	105
Flutter	107
Happy Kitten	109
Hiding Place	111
Dangling Paw	113
Fairy Hat	115
Flower Girl	117
Climber	119
Hello Fairy	121
Goodbye	123

Ice Cream

Butterfly

Swat!

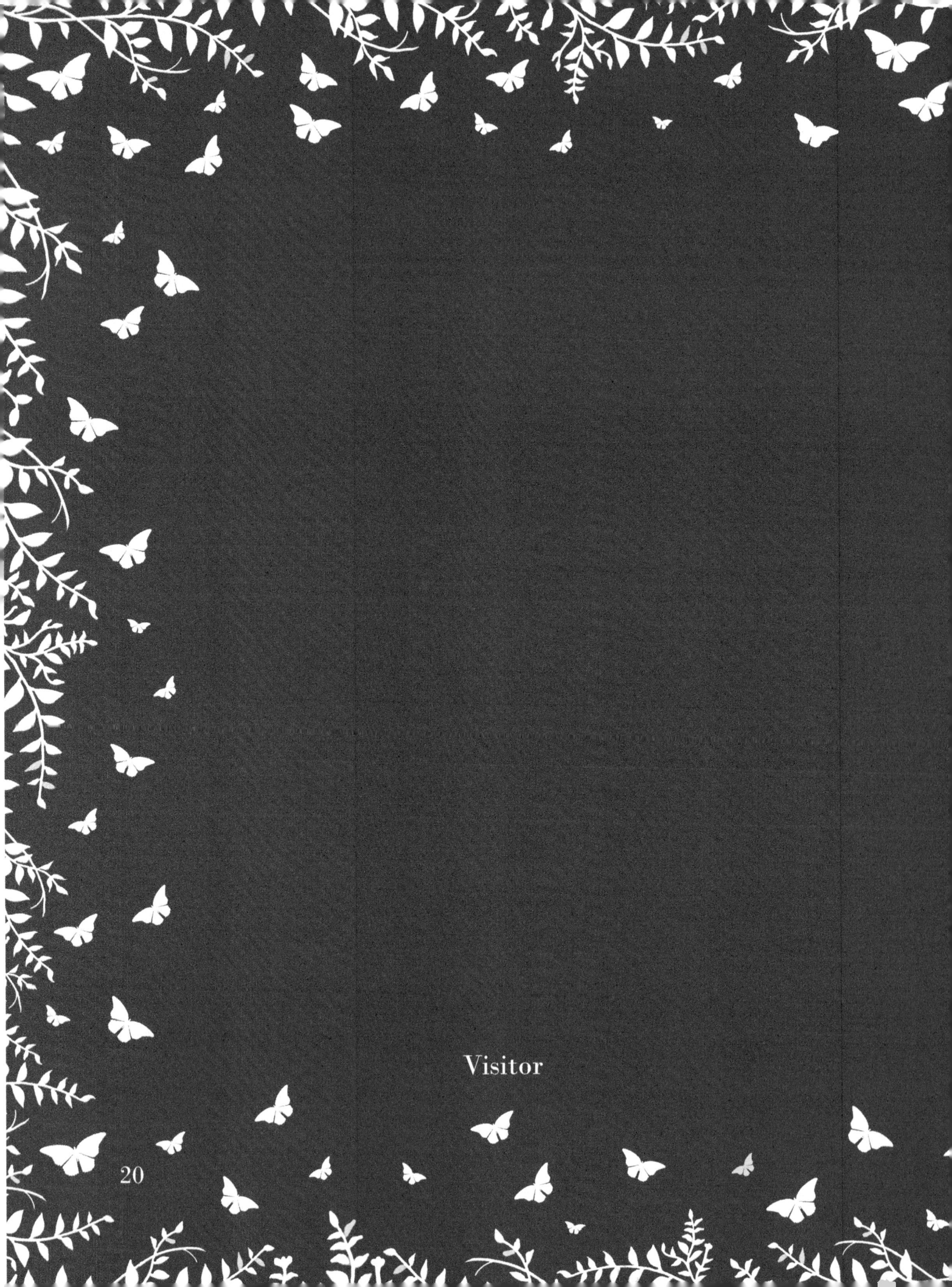

Visitor

Sofa Fairies

Violet Patch

Bath Time

Up in the Air

Hungry Mouse

Bad Kitten

Flower Box

Cheese and Crackers

Slender Branch

Hyacinth Girl

Hanging Around

Swinging

Catch Me if You Can

Jealousy

Fly Away

Kittens Think Oranges Stink

Four Friends

In the Trees

Dragonfly Kites

Wrestling Match

Kitten with Stripes

Climbing Kitten

Pounce

Free Falling

Singing Fairy

Cuddle

Rodent Rescue

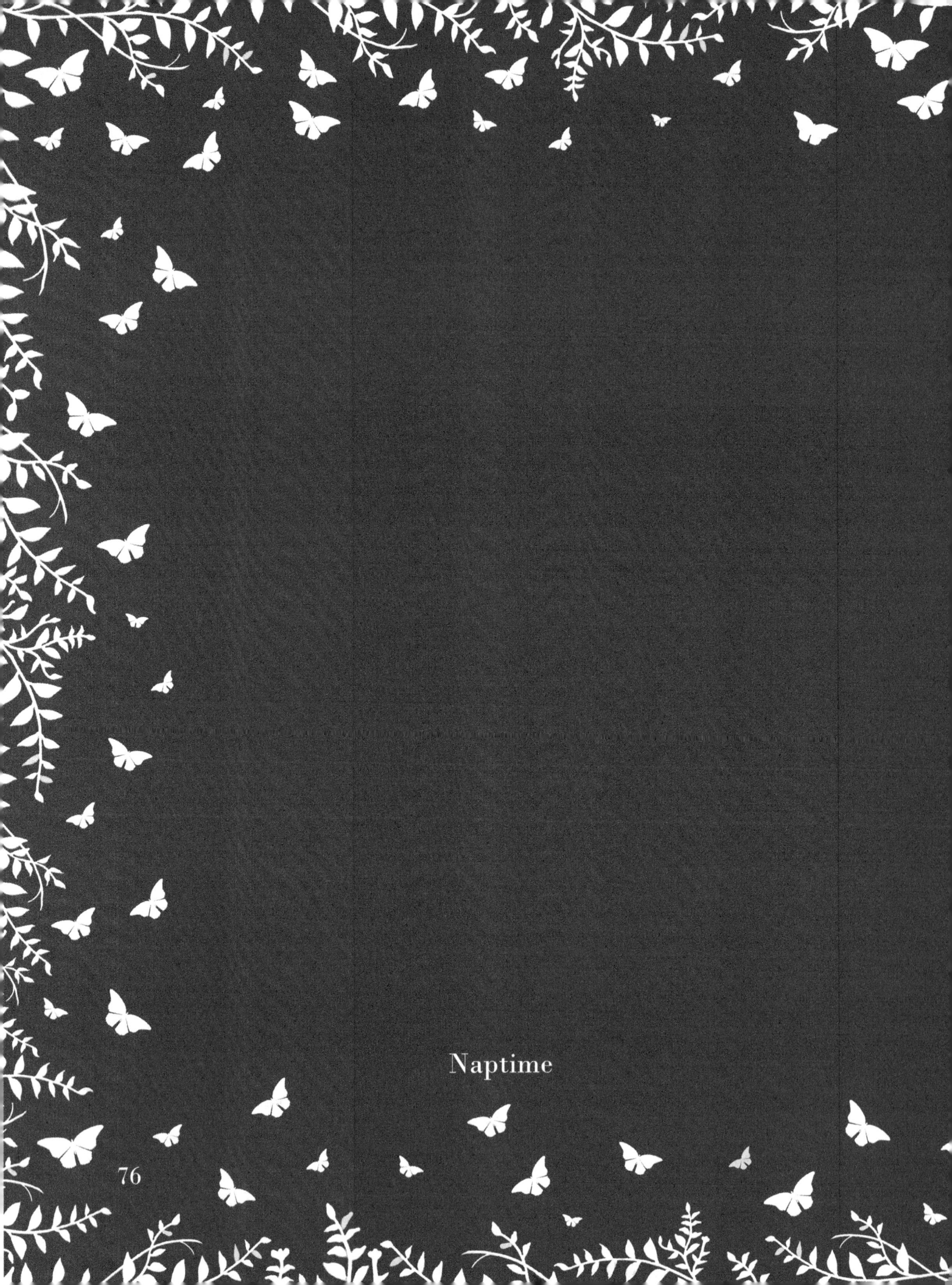

Naptime

String

Fairy Leap

Climbing Buddies

Fashion

Storytime

Silly Fairy

Grumpy Cat

Slide!

What's Up?

Fly Over

Daisy Chain

Tug of War

Kitchee Kitchee Koo

Flutter

Happy Kitten

Hiding Place

Dangling Paw

Fairy Hat

Flower Girl

Climber

Hello Fairy

Goodbye

Made in the USA
Coppell, TX
24 March 2022

75499664R10072